Horses

Children Book of Fun Facts & Amazing Photos on Animals in Nature - A Wonderful Horses Book for Kids aged 3-7

By

Ina Felix

Ina Felix

Copyright © 2015 by Ina Felix

All rights reserved. No part of this book may be used or reproduced in any manner whatsoever without the express written permission of the publisher except for the use of brief quotations in a book review. Image Credits: Royalty free images reproduced under license from various stock image repositories. Under a creative commons licenses.

Hi there! I am Harley, the Horse.

I can be found in woods and farms.

I have four legs and a long tail.

I am very tall. I can grow up to six feet.

I have the biggest eyes among land animals. I can also see at night.

Most of the time, my ears point to the direction I am looking at.

I have big and strong teeth.

I can carry you on my back. I can also take heavy things from one place to another.

I can run very fast.

I can also walk slowly if you want me to.

I can be brown, white, or black.

I like eating grasses, apples, and hay.

I go, "Neigh- Neigh- Neigh!"

I can sleep lying down or standing up.

I can remember things well.

I can identify things just by smelling them.

I can jump so high it feels like I am flying!

I can live up to twenty five years.

My age can be known by counting my teeth.

I like wearing shoes, especially when I am racing with other horses.

I hope you had fun learning about my family.

Thank you.

Made in the USA
Middletown, DE
01 June 2017